Usborne Farmyard Tales

Poppy and Sam's First Word Book

Heather Amery

Illustrated by Stephen Cartwright

Edited by Jenny Tyler

Designed by Helen Wood and Joe Pedley

To listen to all the words in this book read by an English person,
go to the Usborne Quicklinks Website at www.usborne.com/quicklinks
and type in the title of this book. Always follow the safety rules on
the Usborne Quicklinks Website when you are using the internet.

There is a little yellow duck to find on every double page.

Poppy and Sam live on Apple Tree Farm
with their parents, Mr. and Mrs. Boot.

They have a dog called Rusty,
and a cat called Whiskers.

Ted drives the tractor and helps look
after all the animals on the farm.

Poppy

Rusty
the dog

Sam

Mr. Boot

Mrs. Boot

Ted

Whiskers
the cat

Woolly
the sheep

Curly
the pig

There are lots of animals on Apple Tree Farm.

pig   sheep   goat   goose   lamb

cat　　horse　　cow　　donkey　　mouse　chick

5

This is Poppy and Sam's house.

house

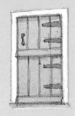
door

roof

chimney

car

gate   window   balloon   bicycle   fence

7

Poppy and Sam are playing by the stream.

frog   fish   haystack   pond   rabbit

tent   path   bridge   scarecrow   boat

9

In the farmyard

Mrs. Boot is washing the **car.**

Poppy is riding her **bicycle.**

Look at the **balloon**!

By the stream

Sam is playing
with his **boat.**

Poppy is sitting
on the **bridge.**

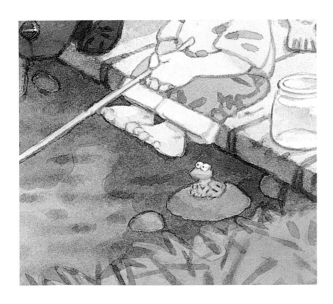

The **frog** is hiding.

A **fish** is jumping out
of the water.

Poppy and Sam are helping to hang the washing.

T-shirt   hat   socks   pants   sweatshirt

jeans   nightdress   sandals   dress   shirt

Poppy is helping Mrs. Boot pick the apples.

tree   fox   butterfly   apple

swing   bee   ladder   snail

15

Hanging the washing

Sam's **jeans** are on the line.

Rusty wants to play with a **sock.**

Poppy is holding her **dress.**

The **cat** is playing with a **hat.**

Picking the apples

Mrs. Boot is up the **ladder.**

Sam is on the **swing.**

Poppy, catch the **apple!**

A **fox** is walking under a **tree.**

Sam is feeding the hens.

 feather  dish  basket bucket  hen

spade   egg   wheelbarrow   hen house   chick

Ted is mending the tractor.

toolbox   steering wheel   rope   spanner   trailer

20

hammer paint tractor seat sack

Feeding the hens

Count the **eggs**.

Sam brings feed in a **bucket**.

One **hen** is sitting on top.

This **chick** is hungry.

Mending the tractor

Ted is mending
the **tractor.**

Sam is holding
the **hammer.**

Poppy is painting the **trailer.**

Poppy and Sam are at the station.

 train

 guard

 flag

 track

 signal

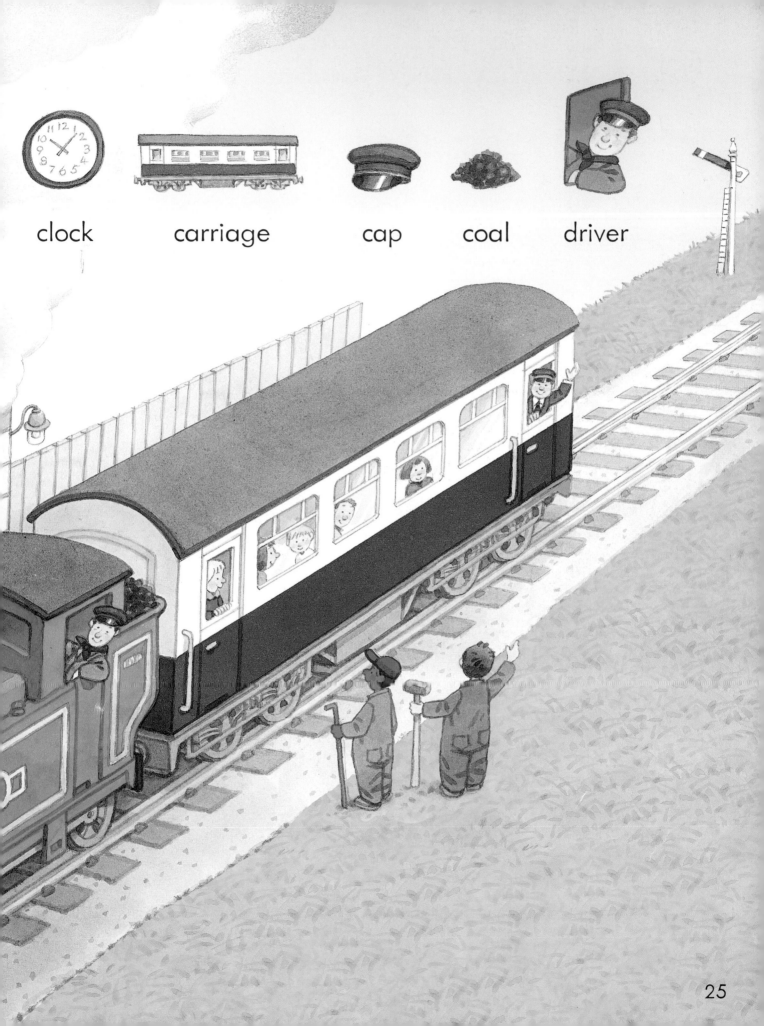

clock   carriage   cap   coal   driver

Poppy and Sam are at the beach.

sunglasses　　towel　　head　　sandcastle　　hand

shell   ball   feet   armbands   crab   ice cream

At the station

There's the **train**.

Mrs. Boot waves the **flag**.

The **clock** shows it's time to go.

The **guard** is smiling.

At the beach

Sam is wearing his **armbands.**

Mrs. Boot is combing Poppy's **hair.**

Mr. Boot is buried in the sand. Only his **head** and his **feet** are sticking out.

Poppy and Sam are helping in the farm shop.

 tomatoes

 mushrooms

 pear

 cabbage

 strawberries

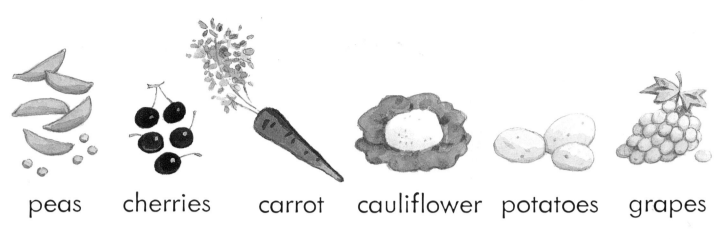

peas   cherries   carrot   cauliflower   potatoes   grapes

Poppy and Sam are having a picnic.

cup

cake

banana

chocolate

yogurt

seven	sunglasses	tree
seventy	sweatshirt	T-shirt
sheep	swing	twenty
shell	table	two
shirt	Ted	umbrella
signal	teddy	wheelbarrow
sink	teeth	Whiskers
six	telephone	white
sixty	television	wind
slippers	ten	window
snail	tent	winter
snow	thirty	Woolly
soap	three	yellow
socks	toilet	yogurt
spade	tomatoes	
spanner	toolbox	
spring	toothbrush	
steering wheel	towel	
storm	track	Can you find a
strawberries	tractor	word to match
summer	trailer	each picture?
sun	train	

rug　　　sandwich　　　umbrella　　　plate　　　fruit juice

In the farm shop

How many **cabbages** is Poppy holding?

Sam has **potatoes** and **lettuces** in his **wheelbarrow.**

Mrs. Boot is picking up a bunch of **grapes.**

Is Curly going to eat the **tomato**?

Having a picnic

Sam is pouring himself some **milk.**

Mrs. Boot has some **cheese** on her **plate.**

Poppy has dropped the **bottle.**

Poppy is reading and Sam is drawing a picture.

camera

picture

newspaper

pencil

photograph

radio   telephone   television   chair   table

37

It's bedtime for Poppy and Sam.

sink   teddy   pillow   slippers   toothbrush   doll

book   mirror   brush   bed   toilet

At home

Dad's reading the **newspaper.**

Sam is drawing a **picture.**

Poppy is reading a **book.**

There's the **telephone.**

Bedtime

Sam is jumping on his **bed.**

Poppy's **teddy** is on her **pillow.**

Poppy is brushing her **teeth.**

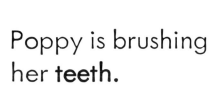

The **soap** is on the **sink.**

Weather

snow

sun

rain

fog

wind

Seasons

spring

summer

rainbow

storm

ice

clouds

autumn

winter

Colours

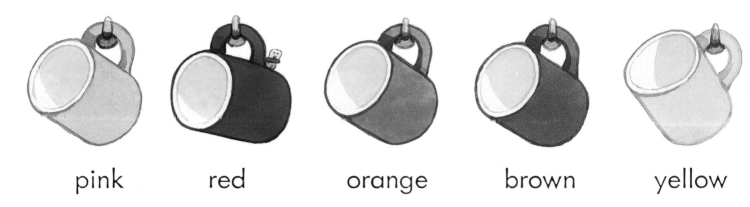

pink   red   orange   brown   yellow

Numbers

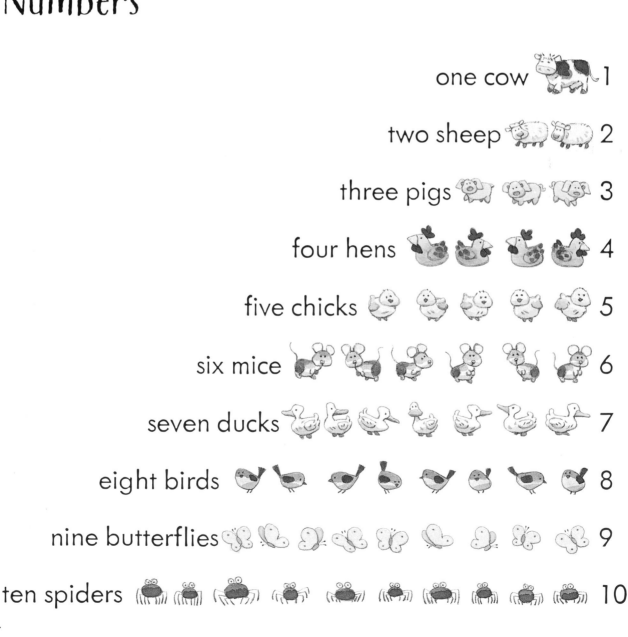

one cow 1

two sheep 2

three pigs 3

four hens 4

five chicks 5

six mice 6

seven ducks 7

eight birds 8

nine butterflies 9

ten spiders 10

green   blue   purple   white   black

There are 100 dogs on this page.

ten	10
twenty	20
thirty	30
forty	40
fifty	50
sixty	60
seventy	70
eighty	80
ninety	90
a hundred	100

Word list

apple
armbands
autumn
ball
balloon
banana
basket
bed
bee
bicycle
black
blue
boat
book
bottle
bridge
brown
brush
bucket
butterfly
cabbage
cake

camera
cap
car
carriage
carrot
cat
cauliflower
chair
cheese
cherries
chick
chimney
chocolate
clock
clouds
coal
cow
crab
cup
Curly
dish
dog

doll
donkey
door
dress
driver
egg
eight
eighty
feather
feet
fence
fifty
fish
five
flag
fog
forty
four
fox
frog
fruit juice
gate

46

goat	milk	pink
goose	mirror	plate
grapes	mouse	pond
green	Mr. Boot	Poppy
guard	Mrs. Boot	potatoes
hair	mushrooms	purple
hammer	newspaper	rabbit
hand	nightdress	radio
hat	nine	rain
haystack	ninety	rainbow
head	one	red
hen	orange	roof
hen house	paint	rope
horse	pants	rug
house	path	Rusty
hundred	pear	sack
ice	peas	Sam
ice cream	pencil	sandals
jeans	photograph	sandcastle
ladder	picture	sandwich
lamb	pig	scarecrow
lettuces	pillow	seat

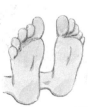